HOW DID YOU GET HIM TO EAT THAT?

12 Parenting Practices That Lead To Healthy Eating

HOW DID YOU GET HIM TO EAT THAT?

12 Parenting Practices That Lead To Healthy Eating

DR. JOHN D RICH, JR.

Lasting Impact Press

Pontiac, Illinois

Copyright 2018 by John D Rich, Jr., Ph.D.

All rights reserved. No portion nor the whole of this book may be reproduced or used whatsoever without written permission from the publisher except in the case of a brief quote included in reviews or critical articles. For information, write to the Publisher.

Title: Positive Parenting
Author: John D Rich, Jr., Ph.D.
Editor: Lisa M. Blacker
Cover Art: Ahmed Moghazy
Distribution: Smashwords
Publisher: *Lasting Impact Press,* an imprint of Connection Victory Publishing Company

    Lisa M. Blacker, CEO & Publisher
    P.O. Box 563, Pontiac, Illinois 61764-0563
    e-mail: info@connectionvictory.com
    website: www.connectionvictory.com

For information about special pricing for bulk purchases, please contact Connection Victory Publishing Company by U.S. mail, e-mail, or phone at 1-630-230-1103.

***

This book is part of a 3-book bundle by the same author to be released on February 10, 2019

Core book:

Positive Parenting: A Practical and Sometimes Humorous Approach To Applying The Research in Your Home With Gender Inclusivity, Mutual Respect and Empathy — and NO Spanking!!

Print (February 2019)

Identifiers: LCCN 2018959033 | ISBN 978-1-64381-011-9 (paperback) | ISBN 978-1-64381-013-3 (ebook) | ISBN 978-1-64381-014-0 (PDF)

Workbook:

Practical Parenting: A Workbook to Accompany Positive Parenting

ISBN 978-1-64381-019-5 (paperback) | ISBN 978-1-64381-022-5 (PDF) | ISBN 978-1-64381-020-1 (ebook)

About the Author

Dr. John D Rich, Jr. is an associate professor of psychology at Delaware State U. His focus is to examine the research about good parenting, effective discipline, and the importance of showing your child warmth and empathy. That research has been instrumental in helping him navigate challenges and rewards of parenting. His experience as a parent, combined with his practice as a researcher in educational psychology, is what he shares in plain language in his new book bundle: "Positive Parenting," the accompanying workbook, "Practical Parenting", and the supplement, "How Did You Get Him To Eat That?"

Subscribe to updates via this case-sensitive link:
http://bit.ly/DrJohnRichCVPubCo

How To Connect With Me

We all strive to be the best we can be in our lives, and we want to raise our children to do the same. To that end, I encourage and look forward to your comments, questions, and insights as this book's circulation grows.

Connect with me here:

    Website: DrJohnRich.com

    Email: info@drjohnrich.com

    Facebook: www.facebook.com/drjohnrich/

    Facebook Group:
    www.facebook.com/groups/1633043126770518/

    Twitter: @Dr_JRich

    Podcast: Dr. John's Neighborhood at ipmnation.com/djn

Thank you for joining me in exploring and thinking intentionally about our parenting.

• • •

Subscribe to updates about the work of Dr. John Rich via his publisher, *Lasting Impact Press,* an imprint of Connection Victory Publishing Company

http://bit.ly/DrJohnRichCVPubCo
(case-sensitive URL)

Table of Contents

About the Author v
How To Connect With Me vi
Introduction 1
1. Begin early 3
2. Buy what you want your child to eat 5
3. Follow the leader 7
4. Be open-minded 9
5. Eat at home 11
6. Keep away from the TV 13
7. Watch portion size 19
8. Consider your parenting style 21
9. Your feeding style influences your child 23
10. Make time 25
11. Get educated 27
12. Healthy eating costs money, but does it really
      cost more? 31
References 47

Introduction

Let's face it. Most kids like Cheetos more than broccoli, and cake more than beans. Give a child the choice between an apple and a cookie - the cookie wins almost every time. I'm the same way. If there were no such thing as calories, cholesterol, and saturated fat, I could eat pizza, French fries, and cupcakes every day. Alas, such a diet will lead to obesity, diabetes, hypertension, high cholesterol, and an early grave [1]. You'll also feel terrible most of the time; you'll have low energy, feel sluggish, and have trouble concentrating.

    We adults have learned the capacity—whether we use it or not is another story—to think about the consequences of our actions, and make choices that trade short-term sacrifices for long-term outcomes. We might choose the carrot over the carrot cake, even though it isn't as sweet, because the carrot is the healthier option.

    Children, on the other hand, are in various stages of learning self-control and delay of gratification. Since human beings seem to be wired to like salty and sweet tastes, and to be prone to avoid bitter and sour tastes [2], children need guidance in their diet choices so that they can choose higher quality foods, in spite of their innate cravings.

    Particularly in the early years, you, as a parent, play an extremely important role in influencing your child's attitudes toward food. You have an impact on your child's food patterns. The way you talk about healthy foods, and the value you place on being open-minded toward new foods are related to how your child will think about healthy options, and how adventurous she will be to try new things. Examples: "Sigh...I guess we better eat this broccoli." Vs. "Oooh! Broccoli!" "That looks nasty." OR "I'm excited to try it." You also have a tremendous impact on your child's repeated exposure to healthy choices every time you go to the store and every time you make a meal. What is your home's ratio of potato chips to apples?

According to two articles [1] [2] about parenting and healthy eating, there are 12 practices and behaviors that are associated with your child's lifelong relationship to food, and his willingness to make healthy food choices when he is older:

1. Begin early.

Food acceptance patterns develop early in life. When children are very young, they will eat whatever is put into their mouths. As they get older, children develop "food neophobia:" a resistance to eating unfamiliar foods. Early and repeated exposure to a wide variety of fruits and vegetables can overcome this neophobia. If they've already eaten it, it's not unfamiliar!

I've heard from many parents who lament how difficult it is to get their children to eat fruits and vegetables. Yet, I've also seen many of those children come to my house, where we have laid out a platter of apple slices, orange slices, pear bites, red pepper strips, and carrot sticks, open their eyes wide, and dive in. The food companies who specialize in sweet and salty foods also specialize in marketing their products. Along the way, they seem to have convinced many parents that children only like to eat junk food and empty calories.

Now, I'm not saying that ice cream and cookies and cheese curls aren't tasty. I'm saying that a child who rarely has any fruits or vegetables is often craving the vitamins and minerals and fiber that those fruits and vegetables contain. If you lay out a variety of healthy and unhealthy foods, your child may gravitate to the unhealthy options, perhaps because these have a more immediate payoff in terms of the high energy and explosive taste that the salt and sugar offer the palette. However, if you lay out snack options that are exclusively healthy, you may be surprised to see your child chowing down.

You can get them started early. After each of my two children were weaned off of breastmilk, my wife discovered a book that I'd highly recommend, called *Super Baby Food*. In essence, author Ruth Yaron offers a convincing argument for feeding babies natural foods, rather than paying for jars of food from the store. Instead of buying jars of Gerber baby food, my wife would take actual fruits and vegetables, steam them, puree them in a blender, and then pour them into ice cube trays. Then, for every meal, all we had to do was put some cubes in a pot and heat them up on a low-medium heat until they melted. No preservatives, no sugars. Just pure fruits and vegetables. And what's more—take it from me, budget-conscious Dr. John—it is cheaper, too.

For that first year, according to Yaron, there's no need to give your baby meat. Focus on mostly vegetables—carrots, spinach, sweet potatoes, broccoli, peas, etc.—supplemented by breastmilk. Don't let your preconceptions about "what kids like to eat" get in the way. A baby who is not even one year old doesn't have food preferences! She will eat what you put in her mouth if she is hungry. This is your best opportunity to make these kinds of vegetables familiar and usual parts of a meal. While you're at it, heat up a couple of ice cubes for yourself, too!

2. Buy what you want your child to eat.

Unless your child can drive or has her own credit card, her food options are limited to what you bring into the house. The answer to the exasperated question, "How do I get my son to stop eating Cheetos?" is "Stop buying Cheetos!" When children get hungry, they want to eat right away. If you front-run their oncoming hunger by placing healthy snacks out on plates, then when they come out for something to eat, they can easily grab what you've prepared. They get to eat and go back to playing, and you get them to eat a high quality snack.

When children are smaller, it's even better if foods are easily accessible (put somewhere that the child can reach) and in easy to eat sizes (carrot sticks instead of entire carrots; apple wedges instead of entire apples). This is what my wife calls the "pre-emptive strike." While your children are playing, cut up some peppers or peaches, put them on a plate, and leave it on a table next to where they're playing. Your children won't need to ask for a snack if they have one available right there. They can absentmindedly graze off of the plate, and you can consciously feel the vicarious pleasure of knowing they are eating nutritious foods.

3. Follow the leader.

Your own beliefs and practices matter. If your children see you eating healthfully, they are more likely to eat healthy foods as well. If your children see you eating cakes, cookies and chips all the time, you can criticize their diet until you are blue in the face. Your lifestyle is a more powerful message than your empty statements. This is entirely consistent with your overall influence as a parent. Your children are taking in how you live in the world, in order to understand how things are supposed to be done. You are one of their only reference points for what is normal.

Now, lest you think I am saying you can never have anything that's not healthy, let me stop you right there. Sweets and salty snacks taste good, and are a nice "sometimes food." A good amount of the research I'm using in this article suggests that, if you restrict a food entirely, you just make it more desirable. The forbidden fruit—or, in this case, the forbidden donut—seems sweeter than the one that is allowed. Desserts are ok to have, but it's better to put restrictions around them. When we serve dinner at our house, there's usually a main entrée, a starch, and a vegetable. If our sons finish dinner, then they can have a dessert. If they are starting to feel full, we don't make them clean their plate, and tell them that they can have dessert if they finish the healthy parts—the vegetables.

I'd like to emphasize that our sons don't even have to do that, but if they don't, then they know they aren't allowed to have dessert. (Later, I'll discuss the importance of letting children stop eating when they are full.) We don't have restrictions on dessert foods—if they want a particular dessert, they can ask for it in time for our weekly shopping trip. We do, however, have restrictions on when those foods are permissible. If you've consistently taught them that dessert happens after a healthy dinner, and you don't allow them to have it unless it is actually after dinner, then they won't ask for it at other times. You've let them have their cake, and they can eat it, too, but only at certain times. These sometimes foods aren't forbidden, but there are limits put around them because they are entirely devoid of quality nutrition. You don't need to say that foods are "bad." You draw the line, and, as long as you stay behind it yourself, they'll respect it.

When they're older, they'll be that much more likely to draw their own lines. We want our children to internalize and understand the reasons why certain foods are limited. As with many other areas of parenting, if we insist on rules "because I said so," or because if they don't, they'll be punished, eventually, when you're not looking, they're going to rebel against your power. Strong-arm tactics often work in the short term, but they do nothing to teach a lesson that your child believes the lesson and will follow it when he is on his own. Talk to your children about the food choices that you make for yourself and your family, so that he makes similar choices when he grows up. Think of it as a legacy that you're giving him—the legacy of how to live a longer, healthier life.

4. Be open-minded.

Your willingness to try new things, and experience different tastes, will rub off on your child. If you are open to spicy foods, your daughter will be open to spicy foods. If you eat it, she will be more likely to eat it. If you make a face when you have to try something different, she will read your cue and hesitate. If you have trouble resisting fast food, or controlling your intake, she will too. There are so many different types of foods, and so many different ways to prepare them. Families who make a determined effort to move toward a healthier lifestyle will have a much easier time if neophobia has been neutralized through an adventurous attempt to try new things.

However, before you just dive in and try something, go online and google "How to make delicious meals with _____." There are so many websites dedicated to great tasting food, with free recipes, which allow you to easily find out how to make your first experience enjoyable. For example, if you decide, "Hm. So many people throughout the world eat tofu, I wonder if I'm missing something," don't just take a package of tofu and cut it up and eat it plain. If it's your first time tasting tofu, I can almost guarantee you will not like it. Instead, go to a website that is focused on providing delicious recipes with tofu, and rely on the experts to show you how to make it pop. Healthy food has the bad reputation of not tasting good, but if you do it right, healthy food can be delicious.

5. Eat at home.

Family meals tend to be healthier, and contain more basic food groups, vitamins and minerals than meals from restaurants. Perhaps because going out to a restaurant is often considered a treat, food selection tends to lean more toward "comfort foods" that have higher fat and salt content. In addition, restaurant meals tend to be accompanied by soft drinks, which have so much sugar and chemicals in them, we would all be wise to avoid them.

When you do go out to eat, consider sharing. The portion sizes in restaurants are often unnecessarily large. You might find that the nachos are enough food for two or three people. This will keep you from overeating, and will also cost less money.

Consider allowing your child to order from the adult menu. "Kids' menus" are notoriously unhealthy. The food is frequently of very low quality, as well. They often offer chicken fingers, french fries, grilled "cheese" on white bread, and burgers. If your children are still very young, you can make them a meal from a few vegetable sides like green beans, apple slices, beets, and corn.

Finally, stay away from soda (fruit juice is no better); the high fructose corn syrup in soda (and juice) is liquefied cancer. If you really have to give them soda, get them a water too. Perhaps you can make them alternate between the soda and the water, finishing both before they can get a refill on the soda.

They may have drunk enough by that point, and they will stop at one glass of cancer.

6. Keep away from the TV.

I don't know about you, but when I'm eating in front of the television, I'm more inclined to eat nachos, burgers, pizza, and sweets than I am salads or fruit. The connection between unhealthy food choices and eating while watching TV may be due to the advertising that we are exposed to: e.g. most advertisements on children's shows are for high sugar foods and fast food restaurants. When I'm watching football, the commercials are heavy on beer, pizza, nachos, and potato products. When is the last time you saw an ad for kale? The more commercials your children see, the more their desire for their products grows, and the more likely you are to buy it for them. Also, you eat *more* when you're watching television because you are absentmindedly eating, not paying attention to how full you feel, or how much you've eaten.

Let's talk about advertising for bit. Open this video on YouTube (https://www.youtube.com/watch?v=xk_hkdGf1tc), and think to yourself, "What associations are these commercials making with their unhealthy products?" As an adult, we often find these commercials silly for how blatantly obvious they are. The use of sex, celebrity, and fun seem glaringly simplistic when we think about them. However, unless you specifically sit down with your child and engage with her about what those messages are, she is not thinking about it that deeply. Without training in how to criticize what she sees, all she sees is what the advertisers want her to see.

Let's begin deciphering the video. What do you see? We begin with a British commercial for a cereal called Weetabix chocolate cereal. Here's a first observation: Chocolate is not a breakfast food! The girl is eating her cereal, and is filled with amazing power. Her teddy bears dance with her to a frenetic song, a genre called "dubstep". She is in sync with the music, and her moves astound her friends. While it is true that the jolt of caffeine and sugar that she ingests in the morning is likely to make her feel energy, the burnout she will later feel when those substances break down is likely to lead to a crash that could very well impact her ability to concentrate in school, and cause her body to crave *more* high energy foods to keep her from falling asleep. The commercial ends with a common claim, catering to the children watching, that eating the product will be fun. "Weetabix chocolate spoonsize…Fuel for fun!" A key question to ask: Is eating *supposed* to be fun? Does it need to be?

Next, we have Reese's puffs cereal. What responsible parent wouldn't advocate eating candy bars for breakfast? More energy and dancing. This teenaged boy is excited to get up, trot down the stairs to the kitchen, which light up as he steps on them (a la the video for Michael Jackson's song Billie Jean), and have a bowl of candy to start his day. While he's eating, he spins his cereal bowl back and forth like a record, in time with the music. This cereal is so fun, it's like being a DJ! The boy's younger brother comes downstairs, and the teenaged boy happily pours him a bowl of chocolate and peanut butter goodness as well.

Backup to a picture of the cereal box, a bowl of cereal, a glass of milk, and a half an orange on a plate. Reese's puffs cereal is described as "an epic part of a complete breakfast." An *epic* part! How great! Even though the cereal has a modicum of vitamins and minerals, it is loaded with sugars and chemicals. The line about the cereal being part of a complete breakfast is sneakily true, in that the orange has some vitamins in it, and the cereal is part of the breakfast that includes the orange. The cereal is *part* of a complete breakfast in the same way that a batch of peanut brittle, supplemented with a piece of fruit is a part of a complete breakfast. The commercial ends with the two boys dancing next to each other, and ending their brotherly bonding with a fistbump. Brings families together!

    Our next commercial is for Lucky Charms. This is the first product that has a mascot, an animated leprechaun, whom the children follow down to a brightly colored cavern filled with brightly colored marshmallows. They grab and eat the leprechaun's cereal, with exclamations of "Yum!" The narrator says that the cereal is "magically delicious." The cartoon character and the bright, primary colors are eye-grabbing for a young child, who will be fully engaged by the rapid camera shifts and attracted to the wide-eyed children who are enjoying the breakfast treat. So far, breakfast has included chocolate, candy, and now marshmallows. Just what your doctor would advise you to eat, first thing in the morning.

    The leprechaun chases them out of the cave because the Lucky Charms the children are eating are his. Apparently, the children have stolen them from his lair. I won't even get into why we're ok with children stealing from leprechauns. The adventures the children have while robbing the leprechaun of his property involve jumping across a path of sugared marshmallows, and running through a meadow of bright green grass. Lucky charms is then shown with a full orange and a large glass of milk, and is proclaimed as "part of a good [but not complete?] breakfast." "Mom, can I have some marshmallows for breakfast?" "Sure, honey, just go down to the leprechaun's lair, and steal some."

The next commercial is for Wildberry Trix cereal. Another mascot, an animated rabbit in a leather jacket, is singing and dancing in front of a swirling screen of bright colors. Again, visually eye catching for a young viewer. The children watching are drawn in by his euphoric and over-the-top antics. He desperately wants some of this cereal, which he describes as "part of a breakfast that's nutritious." (This time, though, there is no picture of any fruit. Just the rhyming scheme.) He can't have any, though. The girl eats her "breakfast," and the rabbit is left without any of the wildberry cereal that we know real rabbits would love. Notice the use of the adjective "wildberry," which suggests nutrition. However, there are no wildberries in the cereal, only flavored sugar.

Next are two commercials for McDonald's. What do we have here to entice children? A clown (Ronald McDonald), a purple monster of some sort (Grimace), a thief (the Hamburglar), a talking box (the Happy meal container speaks and giggles when tickled - how fun!), and the entire CGI cast of the children's movie *The Croods*, which is about cavepeople. They are funny to look at, and stupidly try to eat the McDonald's trays, tables, and chairs. One of them goes to eat a piece of a fern, and an off-camera character says, "That's not food...This is food." And we flash to a picture of a McDonald's meal of chicken nuggets, fries and soda. The character would have been better off eating the fern. At least that's a natural food.

While the happy family eats its collection of saturated fats and carbonated sugar water, and the teenaged boy plays with the cheap "slam bang" toy that came with his "food," we are told that "eating right can be fun when you make balanced choices like milk and fruit in your McDonald's happy meal." The screen briefly shows the nuggets and fries, next to a container of milk and a bag of sliced apples. Same message, right? See it? If I show you a picture of a pile of lard with some apples, I can described the lard as part of a nutritious meal. The child watching isn't thinking this way about what's being said. The implication is that McDonald's is healthy. We all know it's not. At the end, a smiling sloth and three miniature elephants congregate around a smiling Happy Meal box. Friendly and inviting. Oh, and don't forget fun. Gone are the boring days of just eating breakfast to feed your body nutrients.

Soda. There is nothing good about soda. We have to associate soda with good things, because we cannot say it is nutritious. A teenaged boy and girl (are they romantically attached? Unsure) drink from cans of Pepsi. The rest of the world freezes - time stops for them. They roam through the streets as other teenagers are throwing tomatoes at one another with happy smiles on their faces. Seriously - they are for some reason throwing tomatoes at one another. One smiling teenager is about to bite into a tomato. See the association? Tomatoes are healthy, and make you happy. Soda implicitly does the same thing, but even better. The teenagers playing with and eating the tomatoes are frozen, while the soda drinking teenagers get to roam through the city where they find Nicki Minaj in concert. The teenagers get up on stage with her with their soda cans, and then stage dive into the crowd of adoring fans. This is the teenaged equivalent of animated mascots: celebrities with fame and fortune, promising you the same if only you would drink Pepsi!

Another Pepsi commercial promises the same contact with celebrity, but adds sex to the picture. Beyonce pulls up to a gas station (when is the last time you think that happened?), gets out, and walks over to a Pepsi vending machine. We get a slow motion scan of her body, in tight shorts and a belly shirt, while the teen-aged male gas station attendant gapes at her. She slowly drinks her Pepsi, and then looks at the boy with a provocative smile. Obviously the Pepsi has made her horny, and now she wants to sexually exploit a teen-aged male! It's just what Pepsi does! She approaches the boy, and asks him how to get to the interstate. Is this a euphemism? Who knows? All the boy can do is whimper in response.

The final commercial is also for Pepsi. There's nothing new to tell here. We have famous football player Drew Brees and famous boy band One Direction. They are surrounded by fans and, just by their presence, lend endorsement to the soda. Perhaps if I drink soda, I can become a famous quarterback, too? Or, maybe I can be a singer who will be adored by crowds of screaming females? It can't hurt to try, right?

7. Watch portion size.

In addition to the higher fat and lower nutritional value of the food, restaurant meals are also likely to have portion sizes that are excessive. Supersizing your meal as an option, all-you-can-eat specials, and the common attitude that you should "clean your plate" all encourage us to ignore the feeling of being full, and to keep eating. The self-awareness to stop eating when full, and leave any remaining food for a later meal or the trashcan, is only developed with practice, and the permission to do so. At home, use smaller plates and bowls. When you're at a restaurant, divide the food from your order onto salad or bread plates and distribute it around the table.

Many studies have experimentally shown that people will eat whatever is in front of them, and that the amount a person eats can be manipulated upward or downward depending on how much is on the plate. How does this work?

"The amount of food on a plate or bowl increases intake because it influences consumption norms and expectations and it lessens one's reliance on self-monitoring." [3]

If you give your children their meal on smaller plates, and they are still hungry when they are through, put more food on the same plate. Do the same yourself. In many cases, you'll find that you are satisfied with the smaller portion. This is an easy strategy for lowering calories and lowering the cost of your meals without any sacrifice. You'll still feel you've had dinner; you're just manipulating your mind into being content with less food. Something else you can do that accomplishes the same goal is when you order your food, ask for to-go boxes at the beginning and put some of the food in the boxes. You can always take it out if you want more, and the box will keep the food warmer.

8. Consider your parenting style.

Authoritarian parenting, with its focus on the power of the parent and the obedience of the child, is all about control for the sake of control. The authoritarian parent is the style most likely to control a child's eating without regard to the healthiness of the food. A child who misbehaves may be denied supper, or have his Halloween candy thrown in the trash. Alternately, an authoritarian parent may hold out candy or fast food as a bribe in exchange for a behavior.

The permissive parent is most likely to provide little or no structure. Any food that the child wants will be made available, and the child has free reign to eat whatever he wants at any time.

The authoritative parent will encourage her child to eat well, provide reasons and rationales for the food choices that she makes, and provide options for the child, within certain boundaries. As one author states, "[Authoritative] adults determine which foods are offered, and children determine which foods are eaten." This is the parenting style that is most likely to lead to lifelong healthy food choices, because the child has more opportunities to learn about food, and internalize the importance of making good decisions.

9. Your feeding style influences your child.

Certain tropes we learned from our parents, and that they learned from their parents, may unwittingly contribute to unhealthy eating patterns. As mentioned above, "Clean your plate" is the equivalent of ignoring the body's internal signals of satiety. Instead, encourage your child to pay attention to his body, and to stop eating when he's full.

The kinds of foods that you consider snacks are also a part of your feeding style. I remember a commercial not too long ago that tried to convince us that the "3pm slump" we can feel at work should be satisfied with a Red Bull. I cannot honestly think of a worse choice. When you feel that need for a little something to tide you over until dinnertime, what do your children see you grabbing? Almonds, a pear, or a sugary snack? More availability of fruits and vegetables and lower intake of junk foods will go a long way toward teaching your child that it's normal to grab an orange when you're hungry. When your son is a teenager, and his peer group owns a larger share of influence on his behavior, you'll be happy when you hear that he snacks on oranges, and you can do a secret dance to celebrate.

10. Make time.

Meal preparation takes time. Healthy meals may take up to 45 minutes or more to prepare, and often require your complete, undivided attention as you alternate between the meat, vegetable and salad that you are preparing. When you are pressed for time, it's just easier and more realistic to stop at McDonald's or cook some convenience foods (formerly known as "TV dinners"). Making the time to slow everything down is a beautiful practice to prioritize. Sitting down together to eat a meal that was prepared from a unique recipe will create memories.

If you're really pressed for time one day, you can make convenience foods that are healthier by making some whole wheat spaghetti and adding some canned or frozen vegetables. That meal is certainly better than ordering a pizza, and is probably even faster than the drive to McDonald's.

If the problem isn't the occasional time crunch, but a general lack of time for full-on food preparation, try making a bunch of brown rice, browning some meat and roasting a bunch of vegetables over the weekend. Then, you can draw from each of your containers and put a meal together to go into the microwave for a fast and healthier dinner.

Think about fast food for a second. It might take you 10 minutes to drive to your local Burger King, followed by 10 minutes in line, and another 10 minutes to drive home. That's a half hour. Objectively, if you can make a meal that takes you less than 30 minutes to prepare, then the Burger King trip as your quicker option is just an illusion.

Think about it from another angle. The weekend preparation that you do with the rice, meat and roasted vegetables is certainly going to cost some money. Let's analyze how much and compare it to your trips to fast food restaurants. To make enough food to feed four people for five days, your meat might cost you $10, your rice will cost $3, and your vegetables may cost $10. That's $23 for four of you to eat for five days. Alternately, your dinner at Wendy's will cost you $5 each = $20 x 5 days = $100. Fast food only seems cheaper and easier. We haven't even added the amount of time and money you'll spend at the hospital when you have your cardiac arrest!

11. Get educated.

The more education a person gets about how to eat more healthfully, and the benefits of doing so (or the drawbacks of not doing so), the better their choices. If you're looking for some great books about how to make healthy meals for your baby, you might try *Super Baby Food* or *Bringing up Bebe.* If you want to learn more about how to make natural, healthy, and tasty meals for your older children and your spouse, I'd recommend watching the documentary *Forks over Knives* or *In Defense of Food.*

Here's another fantastic trick: Every winter, my wife begins making soups. I asked her to write about how and why she incorporates soup into our family's regular diet. I hope she inspires you to add this cost-effective, healthy option to your own dinner table.

Soup is comforting. Soup is healthy. Soup is delicious. My first soup memories are from when I was very young. Sometimes my mother and I would go out to lunch. My family did not "eat out" very often, and eating out for lunch seemed particularly luxurious - a very special treat. Perpetually health-, weight-, and budget-conscious, my mother usually ordered soup. So of course, I did as well.

When I was 20 years old, I made my first "adult contribution" to my family's Christmas dinner: a relatively simple cream of tomato soup. It was such a huge hit that I was inspired to continue experimenting with soup recipes—primarily vegetable puree-based concoctions with inexpensive and simple ingredients. My family began to give me soup recipe books as Christmas presents, and I greatly expanded my repertoire. Some examples of these early "classics" I still return to are a curried carrot-apple soup, a spicy carrot, a pear bisque, and a cilantro lentil.

I continued the soup tradition once the children came. Soup was great for so many reasons: losing that post-baby weight, an easy way to get vegetables into family meals, introducing new foods and flavors to the children...It is also a great time saver because a big batch of soup can provide lunches, or augment a quick and simple dinner, for days. I can make a big pot of soup on a Sunday afternoon while my husband is entertaining the kids, and then we can have soup and salad, soup and sandwiches, soup and pasta, etc. throughout the week.

Once I understood the basic soup "blueprint" (sauté some onion, add spices, veggies, and stock, boil, simmer, puree), I could concoct my own soups from whatever we happened to have on hand without a particular recipe. This is particularly helpful when we are getting lots of vegetables from our local farm through a community-supported agriculture (CSA) subscription. I have also figured out how to tweak my existing recipes to make them healthier, and vegetarian/vegan (for example, substituting almond milk for cream in a bisque, or switching vegetable stock for chicken).

Soup sounds good even when you don't feel like eating much, but it fills you up. Soup introduces you to many flavors and textures; chowders, bisques, purees, lentils...Soup provides something different or interesting for the palate. If you have a blender, you can make soup. Even a can of peas, blended using only the water in the can and a little salt and pepper, makes a tasty soup that is more pleasurable to eat than just a can of peas. Soup not only provides an opportunity for adding extra nutrition to one's diet, but eating soup with a meal reduces the total number of calories consumed during that meal! [4] *Soup is a great tool to reach your nutritional goals, whatever they may be. You can add a bit of spinach or kale or silken tofu to a soup puree for extra protein or vitamins, for example, and the taste remains unaffected.*

12. Healthy eating costs money, but does it really cost more?

Lower incomes are associated with diets that contain more meat, full cream milk, fat, sugar, cereal and potatoes. These diets also have fewer fruits, vegetables, and whole grain bread. It's difficult to determine exactly how much of these dietary characteristics are due to the price of the foods that are representative, and how much is associated with the relatively lower levels of food education that economically poor parents have. According to the Center on Budget and Policy Priorities [5], the average monthly SNAP (Supplemental Nutrition Assistance Program) benefit for a family of four is $465, which equates to slightly more than $107 per week.

According to a study in 2013 by researchers from Harvard and Brown University [6], "healthier diet patterns—for example, diets rich in fruits, vegetables, fish, and nuts—cost significantly more than unhealthy diets (for example, those rich in processed foods, meats, and refined grains). On average, a day's worth of the most healthy diet patterns cost about $1.50 more per day than the least healthy ones." [7]

For a family of four, this difference amounts to about $2,200 per year or $42 per week. If your benefit amount is only $107, and you have to buy enough groceries to feed 21 meals to four people, setting aside $42 of those dollars for healthy foods may be impossible. Considering the cost of medical treatment and care for people whose diets lead to chronic health problems, it would be worth it to consider policies which opened up opportunities to eat healthier foods, regardless of income obstacles.

However, let's look more closely at the $107 per week allotment. My family of four spends about that much each week, and we eat pretty healthfully. How do we do it? Here are some tips that we use in our grocery shopping that make a $107 per week budget doable:

Buy rice:

At our store, a bag of brown rice that provides 10 portions (2.5 meals for four people) costs 63 cents. That's right. 63 cents! Rice will fill you up, is a good starch to add to a meal, and can be a delicious way to serve vegetables and meats. If we need 7 meals for four people, we'll need enough rice to cover 28 meals. Therefore, we'll need 3 bags of rice. Total cost = $1.89

Only buy foods that are on sale:

This is a general rule that we use in our house for almost anything. If my children want granola bars, they have to pick a brand that's on sale, or wait for them to go on sale before we'll buy it. You really can buy enough food each week if you limit what you buy to what is on sale. There is always a type of cheese, a brand of bread, a size of eggs, and a type of milk (or, better yet, almond milk) on sale. Don't just go with what you've always bought.

Look for the sales and limit what you buy to only those items. Further, keep a list of items when they go on sale, so that you know when the sale that is being offered is a good price, and when the store is offering something as a sale that is really just a few cents off the regular price. You'll become an expert shopper if you pay attention and keep records. If you have a little extra money, and you walk in one day and see something that is a tremendous discount, buy it in bulk**.** The other day, I was perusing the aisles, and I saw that a dozen eggs were on sale for 99 cents. That same dozen eggs is usually $2.99. I bought six dozen. Load up, and then find recipes to cook what you've bought.

The same goes for produce:

Don't buy produce that isn't on sale. The main reasons people think that eating healthy is too expensive are because they are buying junk food that isn't on sale ("I have to have my Doritos!"), or because they are buying fruit and vegetables based on what they're used to buying, rather than limiting their choices to produce that is on sale. *If it's on sale, chances are good it's in season.* Simple supply and demand.

When produce is in season, it is in abundant supply. Stores need to incentivize customers to buy it, because they have so much of it to sell, and so they have to put it on sale. Now, you may want broccoli, but if it isn't on sale, and kale is, buy the kale, and learn how to make it. You may be used to eating oranges for breakfast, but if the peaches are cheaper, go for the gusto and eat peaches for a while.

When fruits and vegetables are in season, they taste better than at any other time. They are also jam packed with more nutrients when they are in season, because that's when God wanted you to eat them. Save the oranges for when they taste best, and go for the peaches when they are the juiciest.

Look for promotional items:

Every once in a while, I will see a little automated machine sticking out from the aisle, pushing out coupons as people pass. Sometimes, those coupons are from new companies who want you to try their product. I recently found some bags of dried fruit from some company I had never heard of. There was a coupon machine in front that said that you could take one for free. Well, free is one of my favorite words. I tried to buy 10 of them, and was told that the coupon only allowed me to buy one. I bought one, then, since the store wasn't busy, I went around and picked another one up and went back in line and got another one. Throughout the week, every time I was anywhere near that store, I went in and got another bag. Dried fruit isn't going to go bad for quite a while, so I knew it would get eaten.

Also, look for special price signs that say that something is on clearance. Not too long ago, there was a brand of salsa, which I suppose was going out of business. They had jars of salsa priced at 88 cents. Salsa is usually $3. Load it up!

Check the unit price:

The unit price is your best guide for getting the best price on an item. Essentially, the unit price is a mathematical way to compare prices for the same item in an "apples-for-apples" kind of way. The price tags on the shelves usually have the unit price on them. Sometimes, an item can be on sale, but the unit price for another brand or size is actually cheaper. Aim to pay the least you can for what you buy, within healthy-food parameters. Don't look at the actual price of the item. Look at the unit price,, and choose the brand and size that has the best unit price. Don't be fooled into buying the 16 ounce container for $2, if the 32 ounce container is $3. By the ounce, the 32 ounce container is the better buy. Usually, the better unit price will be the store brand and/or the larger sizes. Don't be all snobby about what brand it is, and don't be bashful about buying a larger size if you know it will get eaten. Just change what you're going to make that week to whittle away at your larger quantity.

What not to buy:

Not only are sugary cereals a bad way to start your day (eat the other parts of the nutritious breakfast!), they are usually very expensive. Sometimes, one of those brightly packaged boxes of sugar can cost $4-$5! If you want to give your children a breakfast that will be better for them, that won't result in a mid-morning sugar crash, and will provide them with some nutritional value, try this recipe. (My sons calls "the Uncle Jim" because he introduced it to them when our boys stayed at Jim's house) Buy a container of oatmeal (32 ounces costs about $2.75-$4, the cost of one box of sugary cereal). Take one-quarter cup of dry oats, add boiling water, chopped fruit (apples, cranberries, peaches), a tablespoon of peanut butter (if your child is not allergic), and a teaspoon of brown sugar or honey.

Another item I'd encourage you to take off your list are beverages. Don't waste money on juice or soda. Drink water. I know the juice companies have convinced you that juice is healthy, but it's loaded with sugar and is not worth it. Water is what your children should drink. And it's (almost) free!

An example: How to feed your family 21 meals in a week for $107:

The following is an example of a healthy shopping list that can feed your family 21 meals for $107, which will be possible even for a family receiving government assistance. Please note that this list was created in early November 2017, which means that some of the items I am using are ones that would be on sale, and in season, at that time. If you are reading this during a different time of year, substitute the fruits and vegetables with whichever ones you can get for similar sale prices. Also, if I am mentioning a meat or deli item that is on sale, and that meat is not on sale when you go to the store, substitute my selections for those that are on sale at your store, and which are similar in price. This is a guide, not a rule. I am merely trying to show that a food budget doesn't have to be unhealthy to work. If you restrict what you look for to sale items, and in-season produce, you will be able to eat adequately and feed your children healthy choices on a reasonable budget.

Here are the rules I used for compiling this list:

1) I couldn't go over $107;

2) Everyone in the family had to take in at least five servings of fruits/vegetables per day, per the 2005 US Dietary Guidelines of between 5-13 servings per day [8];

3) Everything I bought had to be on sale;

4) Everything had to be easy to make.

In every case, I am creating meal plan for 28 servings of each meal, which is four people, eating 7 days in a week. You'll notice that, if you just drop juice, soda, chips and cereal from your shopping list, your ability to feed your family on a small budget is greatly enhanced. The meals I will describe to you below are affordable, lower in calories than fast food or convenience foods, and I even leave room for snacks or desserts!

Breakfast

In our house, we have two go-to breakfasts that are easy to make, affordable and healthy. The first meal includes 2 eggs (any style), a piece of toast and a half an apple. To make 28 servings of this, I'll need 56 eggs, 28 pieces of bread, and 14 apples. At my store, a carton of 18 eggs was $2.19, so I need 4 cartons, for a total cost of $8.76. A loaf of whole wheat bread was $2.50 for 16 slices, so I need 2 loaves for $5. A 5 pound bag of apples, which has 15 apples in it, is $5.99.

Here's the cost for this breakfast for the week:

Eggs - $8.76
Bread - $5
Apples - $5.99

Total - $19.75! That's less than taking your family out to McDonald's one time!

The other go-to breakfast, "The Uncle Jim," was described above. It is filling, healthy, and even cheaper than the egg breakfast. (You boil some water, add it to some plain oatmeal, add a half an apple cut up in small pieces, and a half a banana cut up in small pieces, and then sprinkle some brown sugar on top. Delicious.)

To make 28 servings, I'll need one 42 ounce container of oatmeal (which has 30 servings) for $3. I need a bag of brown sugar, which costs $1.50 (and has 227 servings, so you'll have extra for next week, and it won't go against your $107 budget). I also need half an apple for each meal, so that's 14 apples, which I can get in the 5 pound bag I discussed above for $5.99, and I need 14 bananas. These are 47 cents a pound, which comes out to 14 bananas for $2.52 cents. Here's the cost for this breakfast if you make it every day for the week:

Oatmeal - $3
Brown sugar - $1.50
Apples - $5.99
Bananas - $2.52

Total - $13.01! Are you kidding me? Takes about 15 minutes to make, and it's tasty, too. Thanks, Uncle Jim!

Lunch

Lunch will be a choice between three sandwiches, and will include a serving of a fruit or vegetable.

The old stand-by, the PB & J, requires 56 pieces of bread (28 servings with 2 pieces each to make the sandwiches). That means I need to buy 4 loaves of bread with 16 slices in each loaf, which cost $2.50 each, for a total of $10. I also need peanut butter. A large jar has 57 servings (which means you'll only use half the jar, and be able to use it for sandwiches next week without it having to come out of your budget), and costs $7.49. I need some jelly. I can get a jar that has 45 servings for $2.50. That's 17 extra servings above what you'll need. Finally, I'm going to splurge and give everyone a pear with their sandwich. That ought to tide everyone over until dinner. Pears are $1.69 per pound this week, which comes out to 85 cents each. I need 28 of them, for a total of $23.80. You could, of course, choose to give your family an apple instead of a pear, which would only cost $5.99 x 2 bags = $11.98. Or, you could buy 7 cantaloupes, which each have four servings in them for $3 each, For $21. But I'm going with the pears for some variety, and also to show you that you don't have to always go with the absolute cheapest things (as long as what you buy is on sale)

Here's the breakdown:

Bread - $10

Peanut butter - $7.49
Jelly - $2.50
Pears - $23.80

Total - $43.79. A little pricey, but will definitely do the trick. Incidentally, if you have access to free or reduced lunch at your children's schools, then this price would drop by half because your children would eat at school, and you and your partner would eat the sandwich and pear combo.

Our second sandwich is a tuna fish sandwich. Each can of tuna is 79 cents, and has 2 servings in it. So, we need 14 cans, for a total of $11.06. We also need to mix it with mayonnaise. A jar costs $3.49 for 60 servings, so you'll have half a jar left for next week, and it won't need to come out of your budget. We need bread - that'll be $10 just like for the PB & Js. Finally, I want a vegetable. I decided to add steamed broccoli. A head of broccoli serves four people, so I need 7 heads. They cost $1.99 per pound, and each head is about a pound, so we're going to call that $14. You can, of course, substitute a different vegetable and probably end up making this cheaper. Once again, I'm trying to mix it up and give a different fruit or vegetable each time I make a meal.

Here's the breakdown:

Bread - $10
Tuna - $11.06
Mayo - $3.49
Broccoli - $14

Total - $38.55. Less money than the PB & J, but you probably wouldn't want tuna fish every day. Perhaps alternate between the PB & J, the tuna fish, and the cheapest sandwich option I can find, which we'll discuss now.

My grocery store has re-tag sales in the meat section every week. Chances are, your store has something similar going on. Chicken breasts are on sale for $0.99 per pound, AND THEN! — Since they are close to being past their "sell-by" date, they have a sticker for an additional 30% off. That is 70 CENTS per pound! When I see something like this, I get teary-eyed because I'm about to rob the bank! I'm not worried about the sell-by date, because I'm going to go to the butcher and ask him/her to separate the breasts into separate wrappings. Since a typical serving of chicken is 3 ounces, two of these large breasts should be enough for a meal for the four of us. So, if I buy a package that has 6 breasts in it, I'll take it to the butcher and ask for it to be divided into three packages with two breasts in each package. The butcher will do so, and then wrap the three packages together with wrap, and put the sticker back on. When I get home, I just take off the wrapper and separate the three packages. I'll put two of them in the freezer, with a note on them in Sharpie to cook immediately after defrosting. The other one will go in the refrigerator, and will be cooked that same day, or the next day at the latest.

That's how you take advantage of the great sales. When I get to the end of this whole meal plan, you'll see that you'll have some extra each week. What you can do with that extra is plan out a dessert for after dinner (which is the only time you will have dessert), or you can use the extra to buy more items that are ridiculously priced for use in a later week. If I have enough extra to buy three weeks of chicken when it's 70 cents per pound, I know that for the next two weeks, I have extra money to use on little side items that make meals more interesting like spices, or condiments, or canned vegetables or canned fruits.

SIDE NOTE: Canned fruit often has added sugar or is in "syrup." This is not the same as fresh fruit and should be treated as a dessert or special snack. Any chance you get to buy non-perishable stuff that you can use later, you should do it. This gives you leeway for holiday meals when you might want to spend a little extra on tradition, or the occasional comfort food that you want to have around.

Back to our final sandwich: chicken salad. Now, they do make canned chicken, right next to the canned tuna, but it will cost you $21 to buy enough for 28 servings, and plus YOU'LL BE EATING CANNED CHICKEN. Personally, I'd rather have fresh chicken. Since 3 ounces is a serving, that means I need 3 ounces x 28 servings = 84 ounces of chicken, or 5.25 pounds. In my picture, you see I found two packages, which weigh 2.84 pounds and 2.59 pounds, which adds up to 5.43 pounds. That will cost me $3.80. Holy Toledo! A week's worth of chicken for $3.80! If that doesn't excite you, you'd better check your pulse.

Next, I need my bread for $10, some mayonnaise for $3.49, and then I'm going to add some spinach, which you can steam or sauté in butter (this is included in the budget for the dinners below, so it's not included here). Each pound of spinach has four servings, and costs $1.50 per pound. So, 7 pounds will cost $10.50.

Here's our breakdown:

Chicken - $3.80 (WOW!)
Bread - $10
Mayo - $3.49
Spinach - $10.50

Total - 27.79

Dinner

Our final meal of the day will include a protein, a canned vegetable, some steamed carrots, and some rice. Rice is your cheapest way to get a starch and fill out the meal. Let's work through it. Our protein could include chicken again. We already know that will cost $3.80.

If you're having chicken for lunches this week, you might want to have sausages for dinner, instead. I can get a package of 16 sausages for $3.99, so I'll need two packages which will cost $7.98. Another option is possible because, at the time I am writing this, Thanksgiving is around the corner. If you buy a turkey that is at least 10 pounds, you can get it for 49 cents per pound. This is even cheaper than the chicken. So, if I buy a 10 pound turkey, that will cost $4.90, and I'll have quite a bit extra for turkey sandwiches, soups, or casseroles. Since we probably can't find a turkey that was nice enough to weigh exactly 10 pounds, let's round this number up to $5.50. Next, we have canned vegetables. I'm not sure why people shy away from them. I know they're not fresh, but they're still healthy, and can be bought in bulk when and if they come up for a deep discount.

This week, canned vegetables are on sale for between 79-99 cents per can. There are, to name a few, cans of beets, green beans, corn, peas, and carrots. We'll price these at 99 cents per can, just to be conservative. Each can has 3.5 servings, so we need 8 cans for the week, for a total cost of $7.92. We're also going to buy some fresh carrots. I can buy a 5 pound bag of carrots, which will more than cover our dinner plan for the week, for $2.99 (By the way, a one pound bag is 99 cents, which would cost almost $5 for 5 pounds. It's almost always cheaper to buy bigger sizes. Unit prices are your friend!).

Finally, we need some rice. The bag of rice with the best unit price has 50 servings in it (so you have some left for next week), and costs $2.79. To this meal, I'm going to add an onion (which will cost $1.13 for a 12 ounce size at $1.49 per pound) and some butter (cost is $2), both of which can be used throughout the week for making vegetables, sandwiches, eggs, or even cooking the apple slices that we'll put in the "Uncle Jim," which taste heavenly when cooked with butter and brown sugar.

Here's the breakdown:

Meat - $3.80 for the chicken, $8 for the sausage, $5.50 for the turkey
Canned vegetables - $7.92
Carrots - $3
Rice - $2.79

Total - $17.51 for the chicken dinner, $19.22 for the turkey dinner, and $21.71 for the sausages.

Let's tally it all up.

Let's just go crazy and add up the most expensive options for all three meals, so that we can be sure we're going to be able to afford what we've planned. Of course, the more you buy things that leave you with leftover ingredients, the more capable you're going to be to add more variety to your menu. For now, let's just pretend that we're going to have the egg breakfast, the PB & J sandwich, and the sausage dinner every day of the week. These are the three most expensive meals that we've described, so if we can afford those, then using some of the other options throughout the week will be even cheaper.

Here's our total budget:

Breakfast - $17.56
Lunch - $43.79
Dinner - $21.71

Total - $83.06

Time to do a dance! Remember, we have $107 to spend. We still have $24 leftover, and we've eaten great tasting food, with healthy ingredients, and can now think about how to spend our extra. Don't forget, this is the biggest amount of money for what we put together. You'll probably choose to do different sandwiches for lunch, rather than all PB & J. You'll most likely want something different than sausage every night, and I'm sure I wouldn't want eggs 7 days per week. So, you're more realistically going to end up with a larger surplus than the $24. Let's just go with that amount, though. What can you do? Well, you can buy a whole bunch more chicken, or a bigger turkey, since the price is currently very low. Or you could stock up on canned fruits and vegetables. Or, you could buy some spices, or give yourself a treat for a job well done—maybe you buy a bag of Doritos to have during the football game this week.

Or, maybe you want to be able to provide dessert every night, or a midday snack every day, or give everyone the choice to add one extra bit of food intake in the afternoon or the evening (but not both). Here are a few snack/dessert options you can consider:

Pumpkin cupcakes. Perhaps this doesn't sound good, but just try it. They're so moist, they're so easy to make, they are healthful, they sneak pumpkin (a superfood!) into your children's stomachs without them even knowing, and they are truly delicious. You buy a box of chocolate cake mix, and you mix in a can of pumpkin. That's it! No eggs, oil, nothing. Just pour the two together, put the mix in a cupcake tin (or a pan if you don't have one) and cook for the amount of time on the box.

How much will this cost? Each box of cake mix has 10 servings, so we'll need 3 boxes to last the week (In fact, the serving size is for slices of cake. So, when you make cupcakes, you'll probably end up with twice that amount. Still, in the spirit of being conservative with our money and serving sizes, we're going to calculate this using the 10 servings as indicated on the box). The boxes of cake mix cost $1.25 each, and we need 3, so that's a total of $3.75. Each can of pumpkin is $1.99, and we need one can for each of our three boxes, so that's $5.97. And then, if you want icing (which is really unnecessary, but let's go for the gusto!), you'll need three containers, which are currently on sale at 3 for $5.

Here's the breakdown:

Boxes of cake mix - $3.75
Pumpkin - $5.97
Icing - $5

Total - $14.73. Pretty good. We still have a little more then $9 left.

How about carrot sticks? Make your own. Buy the 5 pound bag, skin them and cut them into smaller sizes, for $3. How about 12 pears? $10

Here's another snack: Buy 3 boxes of Triscuits (the store version is $1.50 each, for a total of $4.50), a jar of tomato sauce, which I can get for $1.25, and 2 bags of shredded cheese, which are $2 for an 8 ounce bag. These amounts are all enough to have a serving for each person all week. Total? $9.75.

Feel free to alter any of this to suit your taste, interest, values, or preferences. The big idea is this: If you plan it out, shop smart, and pay attention, you can eat healthy food, on a budget, without sacrificing taste. Mix and match - make the snacks the lunch and the lunch the snack. Have eggs for dinner, and the sausage dinner for lunch. It doesn't matter. Plan out your meals for the week, create the budget so it is affordable, and then, when you go to the store - ***don't buy anything that is not on your list!!!***

If you are fortunate enough to not need such a strict budget, consider the possibility of spending more money on higher quality, healthier foods. According to two recent studies [9], [10], Americans spend a much lower percentage of their household budgets on food than many other countries, and also a much lower percentage than their grandparents' generation. The diet you feed your family is a basis for their physical and cognitive development. Filling your home with more fruits and vegetables communicates the value you place on healthy eating, and will pay numerous dividends as your children mature.

Like anything else with parenting, your choices, actions, and attitudes are the raw material for your own child's later relationship with food. We sure did take on a lot when we agreed to be parents, didn't we? In spite of all there is to do, and do well, it is a privilege that you can look back on with pride.

References

[1] Taylor, J. P., Evers, S., & McKenna, M. (2005). Determinants of healthy eating in children and youth. *Canadian Journal of Public Health/Revue Canadienne de Sante'e Publique*, S20-S26.

[2] Benton, D. (2004). Role of parents in the determination of the food preferences of children and the development of obesity. *International journal of obesity*, *28*(7), 858.

[3] Wansink, B., Painter, J. E., & North, J. (2005). Bottomless bowls: why visual cues of portion size may influence intake. *Obesity*, *13*(1), 93-100.

[4] https://www.sciencedaily.com/releases/2007/05/070501142326.htm

[5] https://www.cbpp.org/research/a-quick-guide-to-snap-eligibility-and-benefits

[6] Rao, M., Afshin, A., Singh, G., & Mozaffarian, D. (2013). Do healthier foods and diet patterns cost more than less healthy options? A systematic review and meta-analysis. *BMJ open*, *3*(12), e004277.

[7] Quote from Marge Dwyer in an article found at https://www.hsph.harvard.edu/news/press-releases/healthy-vs-unhealthy-diet-costs-1-50-more/

[8] http://healthyeating.sfgate.com/many-fruits-veggies-should-eat-day-3324.html

[9] https://www.npr.org/sections/thesalt/2015/03/02/389578089/yo

ur-grandparents-spent-more-of-their-money-on-food-than-you-do

[10] htttps://www.vox.com/2014/7/6/5874499/map-heres-how-much-every-country-spends-on-food

www.ingramcontent.com/pod-product-compliance
Lightning Source LLC
Chambersburg PA
CBHW070801050426
42452CB00012B/2447